The Sorrowing House

The Sorrowing House

GENEVIEVE LEHR

Brick Books

National Library of Canada Cataloguing in Publication

Lehr, Genevieve, 1956–
    The sorrowing house / Genevieve Lehr.

Poems.
ISBN 1-894078-36-5

I. Title.

PS8623.E47S67 2004   C811'.6   C2004-903122-8

We acknowledge the support of the Canada Council for the
Arts, the Government of Canada through the Book Publishing
Industry Development Program (BPIDP), and the Ontario
Arts Council for their support of our publishing program.

The cover is after a painting by Heidi Oberheide, "White Bird
& Figure," acrylic on canvas, 34 inches x 44 inches.

The photograph of the author was taken by Dave Panting.

The book is set in Minion and Chaparral.

Design and layout by Alan Siu.

Printed and bound by Sunville Printco Inc.

Brick Books
431 Boler Road, Box 20081
London, Ontario N6K 4G6

brick.books@sympatico.ca

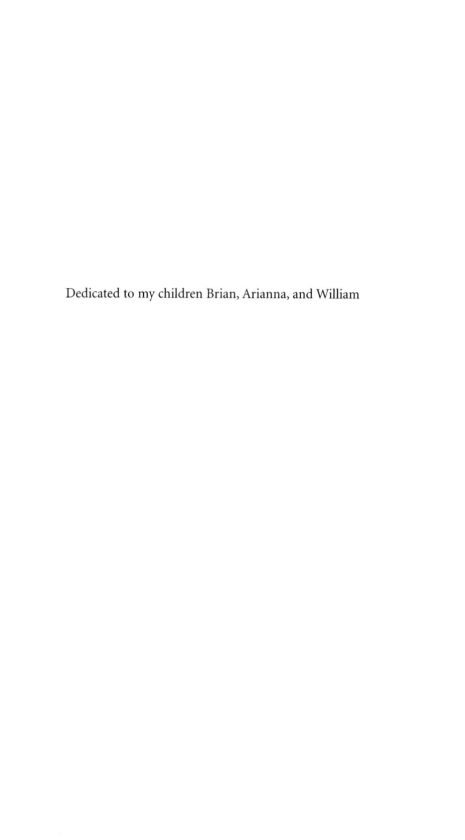

Dedicated to my children Brian, Arianna, and William

🌿 Metaphor for the Design of Wings

🌿 Repertoire of Longing

🦎 Winter Songs

❧ Afterimages

Metaphor for the
Design of Wings

Hummingbirds

How far they travel. The distance of a lifetime.
The Ruby Throat will fly two thousand miles
non-stop across open water. Could you love
this much?

The hummingbird comes. She throws
her head back, hovers, dips the slender amphora
of her mouth into sugar water I have prepared for her.

Then there is the hummingbird of dreams.
At the window she is a winter bird, her breast
reddened with need, her heartbeat measured
by the stillness the air leaves behind.

Crows

Crows come first. Always
the first up.
I murmur something about a song and a feather
falls. Black of course, so black it blossoms, becomes
my face, a puddle of rain.

Crows describe daylight, traffic,
weather conditions.
They gather close to my window, their mouths
are jars morning tumbles from
dishevelled
and slow.

In their conversation they explain
the warmth of asphalt,
freezing
rain in the high branches of pine, the dream
I have wandered out of
searching for clues.

This is the way stars see, they tell me,
their hearts spun out to infinity.
And the way back?

If I follow them, more rain will fall.

Placement

The phone rests in the palm of her right hand.

At the table she observes a fly move across a page.
Paper with its snowy cheek, the epilogue.

Outside, light follows the wind
over new spring grass —
his mother's hair, seaweed blown back,
air tinged with the odour of rust.

First there is a form you must fill out.

She crosses a landscape
where light can at any moment
disappear, become
water, the roots of trees
grown underground
surfacing
under a miner's lamp.

On the first page there is a box
in the upper right hand corner.

She has dreamt him into light:
her son.
His heart is a filament of flesh,
the frond of a Precambrian world,
spored at the water's mouth.

Dotted lines are a cluster of stars. Nebulae. A place to sign,
thought diffused at the moment of breaking off.

Her face is refracted like the sea.
She finds his image in water,

and the table she lays her head upon
is the heart of a spreading forest.

Age. Date of birth. Reason for placement.

It is as if an entire century has gone by.
As if the fly goes on contemplating the same
anguish, and the house around her dissolves
from the roof down.

Wheelchair. Insert. Headrest. Footrests.

Snow is falling away from the hillside.
Below, she watches a man, his boat,
the line he brings her laden with
invisible fish.

⊚⊚

He will be given away like faith.
At Easter, the elders gathered.
A line of pews, palms spread out.

House of bondage.

The smell of a stationary body
is the odour of newly butchered
meat. Fear imbues living tissue
with the scent of its own confinement.

I will lead you out.

It is inside her, in the lining of her nostrils,
in her gut.

The phone is falling from her hand.
His hand is translucent like porcelain.

He tumbles through the air
with wheels of cold silver.

◉◎

Light enters stone the colour of ocean.

He tumbles through the air
with wheels of cold silver. She brings him back,
and the water she peers inside
shuts her into silence.

My son I am building a house
where you and I will live forever.

In the photograph, his hand
brushes the incubator wall.
The wind falls.
A mother breathing
in sleep.

I am turning the pages
of a hundred books
that sing while you sleep.

Outside, the old moon is visible in the daytime sky
where trees touch
with thin, startled hands.

I am telling an old story,
one circled by the moon; faces
appear that do not speak

but I know you will be listening
long hours into daylight.

༺༻

His name follows after her, inquiring:
what is in us that has been changed forever?
Morpheme, phoneme, thought?

Is it the immensity of planets,
or the collapse of latitude
as we navigate interior seas?

She carries him alone into sleep
down a highway woven from the darkness.

He is mystified by the night, the hem of her grey coat,
the white tower of her hand closing over his.
It is past midnight. They travel upriver.

I will lead you out.

His body is the touchstone where rivers meet,
it is a compass leading the wind.

Her son is heavy in her arms,
the bulk of paper, the blank white
form.

༺༻

My son, I cannot carry you.

Portrait of My Son

My imagination shapes you, takes inside it what the river has
done, feels your heart with its tiny, dimpled nodes. First, you
are an embryo with a yellow mane. The other theory, the
sacrilege that exiled Galileo into parts of himself which only
his small daughter could find, explains those darknesses even
the innocent carry with them. *The letter, papa,* she said, *read
the letter.* All stained: sunspots, a father's lonely tears.

I shape three loaves of you, braid your face, stretch and pull
until you are formed with a wisdom only the river can know.
Ice begins to shift, breaking under bridges, stopping two feet
away from the house you have come to spend the night in.
You are born again to stand upright, reach into fire for the
branch your father has asked you not to burn. That branch
of truth, he said, the destiny of an unnamed tree.

Before me, the hands of a child with palms barely opened.
His feet are washed by a woman who crosses a bridge only to
discover the son she worships is walking lonely on the other
side. There is another way, I explain, an equilibrium found
only by sitting still or digging in the earth with a stick, where
for centuries ants have worked, teaching the planets their ten,
masterful harmonies.

Now, you open outward, sticky with light. If I give you feathers,
the air will take you from me. Instead, I'll give you a chair to
pull up before a fire, gloves to warm your still, white hands,
a face that moves like a river as it cuts through granite gorges
pulled seaward by Kepler's faithful moon.

The Letter

On the first line
the juvenile quarterlies
of the moon appear —

hieroglyphs shaped like a cat's ear
(meaning a cat's ear)
the Chinese character for love
and adoration ...

I have a sense of you
here in a wedge of sunlight,
the backward weight of your shadow
heavy as a cat's paw.

What touches me here,
this stirring?
Is it the river rolling away
or syllables with their uvular
hearts shut up in stone?

The metre of thought
is the hexagram meaning
alone;
the salutation, a trochee breathless with love.

How long you have been gone, I write.
How desolate the wind. How long you have been gone.

Goldfinch

The children found you first. One eye open, feathers
yellowy smooth and folded just the right way
for death. I believed for a moment
you were not dead. But the wind knew,
certain with the weight of so much emptiness.

The face of a sleeping bird is a parable
the wind tells. As I listen, the children carry you
in a wicker cage up the hillside. My son gives you
a cross. They name you Elvis. And sing.

It is singing as Darwin first heard it.

I watch them disappear into sunlight, their faces wreathes,
their bodies lupines and irises
that bow with the solemnity of ushers.

Tree Life

There is a moss-covered canoe under the bark of a sequoia tree. The living heart of a bird is placed, still throbbing, upon the swollen feet of a prince to ease the pain of gout. Each part of the tree, down to roots whitened by mud, knows that when the essence of the heart is rendered, a seed leaves the branch, goes wandering, becomes a ship in a conqueror's hand.

Chairs around the table look back over their long life, the families they've grown into, conversations they've heard that only birds would understand. Their old home was an essay on managing a forest, and before that something darker, the earth perhaps, which had whispered its billion secrets into their tiny, blossoming ears.

I walk around the table shaped from a Newfoundland pine. It is long, with symmetrical lines that converge, then move outward to give the kitchen light. The name of the builder is known only to the burrowing knots that winter made in the tree's moist flesh. Did he talk of how he loved her, the marriage to come, sing to the pine's heart those lonely hours shaping stakes and dowels to keep the table together?

No matter how long we live here, shaking sawdust from our hair, listening to chainsaws, handsaws, or the carpenter's gentle plane, the wood we touch is an orphaned tree prepared to walk through fire to go home.

House

Perhaps this is the house in which I lived
when neither I, nor earth, existed,
when everything was moon, or stone, or shadow,
with the still light unborn.
Pablo Neruda

It was born in me. The light on one side. Stars scrambling
for the roof's peak. The chimney rises up like a wave, then
withdraws a little, settles into its new foundation. Occasionally
there are voices in the kitchen, laughter, someone in a blue
dress peeling an onion.

My palm is a door leading into other rooms that haven't been
opened for years, light with its pallor of sky. The funeral of an
old aunt who died while planting peonies near the pond; she
could sing gravesongs to make the furniture weep. I enter a
garden where I am a stepdaughter who'll fall down a well to
recover treasures of lost gold. And then be rained upon.

The house fits inside my pocket now, it will flatten, stay calm
whenever I enter a cave where darkness is imminent, old
tentacles of shame still clinging to the moon's feet.

School

As if day had come with an institution of its own,
you appeared at a window all
alphabets and half-made hats.

A bannerless wind bore you there, wheels
strapped down, arms and body stiff as
September air.

It was a day of overtures and tears.
A day when autumn came,
poetry, the exuberance of a leaf.

The bell rings, the wheels of your body
turn.

For your sake, children make wheels
to fill the sky. Ixion exiled for love,
mill wheels and boats paddling bravely downriver.

Let's name everything in the sky, they say,
their faces comforted by the planets' infinite whispers.

O phenomena of water. The stars once named
become keepsakes, faint echoes of stone, the way
we disappear into firelight and are forgotten
for centuries.

◎◎

The birth of a soul is the world begun again.
It is the sky alive with rain.

The principal is uncomfortable in the silence, her face
is a thinning pocket emptied on the roadside.

The droop of my son's back,
wheels beneath him brimming with light. His face
a book of stars,
wind filling a sail on the equator's rim.

The child before her searches the walls
of an incubator,
finds the 'I' of his name, climbs
the roof of its sound.

⊚⊚

The horse he rides nuzzles the fence.
Spurs spin, wheels of cold silver.

There is a parable resting on his tongue.
Children waiting to touch.
Light-years of change dancing through his teeth.

⊚⊚

The voice of the mother is calm, a gentle nest
blackbirds shaking their feathers against the cold.

Silver, colour of absence.
The moon with its clear, polished surface.

The spokes of a wheel are roads
leading inward, a mandala of light.

At a table, as in a circle of stone,
each hand laid down
offers its own truth. Teachers, social workers,
papers grown thick with age,

rheumatic pens,
the flashing charts of a chemist. The principal begins.

A child, he tells her,
is known by the object touched,
a coin misplaced.

Papers shuffle. Chairs.
She bows her head in the uncertainty,
imagines equations, the darkness of space,
the outline of her own face,
eccentric and alone.

Yes, she says, *O yes*.
The religion of loss.
Taller than a flame.

◎◎

She pulls on red leather boots.
A coat. Morning in grey cashmere.

The eaves of a house heavy with new frost.

They wait together. A small eternity.
A minute, day, year?
A porch light warming the morning with its lonely equipage.

There are five directions the fingers seek.
But what of the highways of the face, the waterlines?
The riverbanks dishevelled by moonlight and sleep?

In another city, there are rooms with hallways held together
by the hands of a clock. Seasons, days of the week
the way we number "infinite" and "empty". The exact
set of all things.

John

A man who has made a pilgrimage to Spain teaches my son.
Law, he says, is a principle of mass cohesion or a simple
listening *to* when rivers heave wildly, abandoning their
books. His name is John, an emanation. He explains that
to build a house on sand is to understand the force of three
tides, or the ecstatic life of a Hermit Crab that, at the end
of a long day, goes home faithfully to itself.

He knows the moon and her faces, the one that turns
completely away from you, and the one, like my son's, whose
light leans down and aches toward growing. On a mountain
road in Spain, a man, plaintive because his donkey had
struck his foot on a cactus and stumbled, recited love poems
in the donkey's ear. *Platero,* he said, *when you are no longer
with me, who will climb the mountain to bring blackberries
and carnations from the crazy girl Aguedilla's house?*

In school, the silences are kept in a room for my son to hold.
He embraces great distances, their dimensions, the weight of
so much knowing. John opens his gospel of kindness, reads
aloud the Periodic Table to honour the earth, reveals the
inner voice of Relativity. A wheel, for instance, expands at
the rate of the human heart in its deepest sorrow. When we
move forward, the spokes multiply and bend into Mesozoic
birds newly arrived from the sea.

Song of the Beloved

i

The father he loves collapses the empty wheelchair, folds
down the house. Gone for another while.

These times together, the father thinks, have softened the
light the sun lets in from the sea. The chair his son wheels is
a Russian short story where a man is lost hunting but doesn't
perish. The father arranges his own astrology, is quieter now,
speaks more languages than he ever remembers learning. He
and his son tell old stories and nudge the air, comrades.

There was a woman who went mad because she could not
wash her dead husband's hair, pressed her cheek upon a pane
of glass to comfort the sorrowing house. If she had only
waited, the father begins to explain. Strums a note. Sings into
the sky, the guitar's blue surface where an echo journeys into
the wilderness to summon itself home.

The folded chair is another language the father teaches his
son, sings of its components: the silver wheel with its
apocalyptic spin, the hands joined to a constellation of the
hunter, legs on footrests that pivot and swing away.

Is it possible to endure the wheel's song, the mud-filled
tracks left by a caravan of gypsies whose singing had taken
his son away? The song wears a red shirt, speaks of rivers that
lose their way, of children who love too much, and an island
in the Atlantic where a house is shaking in the dream of
another wind.

ii

The strings of his father's guitar are junctures, old regrets, the
way leaving takes us in its arms and we weep for a home that is
fifty fathoms down. There is poetry in his stride, attenuated
form.

The framework for truth is this: a man pencilled lightly inside
a wheel, his hands approaching the vertices of the square.

The wheels his son rides upon are melted-down moons,
festooned with the tailings of stars. The father sees the eyes of
a boy learning how not to walk, how to sit quietly, observe the
long hours of the world in the tapestry of an empty street.

Sometimes, the woman who is mad as rain lifts her cheek from
the pane of glass and listens in. A ballad comes to her, the shoe
of a drowned wanderer scraping the gravelled walk. Her face is
a story told around a fire, in a room where strangers gather with
maps of continents and ocean floors.

The father he loves collapses the empty wheelchair. Folds down
the house. The chair, he explains, is a metaphor for the design
of wings, for the true rotation of the planets, the orbits, the sun
that lives inside itself and burns from the sky, unmoving.

February 15, 2002

Thirty days hath September, I recite brushing the mud from
the wheels of your chair, late autumn sunlight melting the
half-formed earth that holds you up. *April, June and
November.* Snow comes. You skid in ruts made by an early
builder, a wheelwright who settled along these shores after
his ship had run aground. In his arms he carried his son,
broken by the keeper's light. His wife hung curtains at
midnight to drown out the sounds of the unsettled tides
swaying in the moon's embrace.

All the rest have thirty-one. I spend days reminding myself of
small equations, the distance from one star to another, the
length of a raindrop with its elliptic side split by glass. The
number of hours I want to live for you, down to your life's
one breath, are tallied and crossed off in tens. By firelight,
you count the notches made in the centre of each flame,
a diviner who deciphered markings made by fire on the
scapula of a deer. *A mark in the centre means starvation,*
you said, *no more paths to follow.*

Excepting February alone. When the Ocean Ranger listed, the
time of a man's final breath was held on the crest of a wave.
Eighty-four notches in flame. You look up and see the space
inside me widen, the oil rig facing a hundred-foot seas,
mountains not yet crossed that settled in me years before
you were born.

Which hath but twenty-eight, in fine. I teach you what is
unremembered, the way a flame will leap into the image of
your face, your father singing over you, naming the days,
weeks, the chords of a song ringing under his tired hand. The
stories I read are numbered like indrawn breaths, or dream
maps your father carried to exemplify the deerslayer's hymn.

'Til leap year gives it twenty-nine. Time can also be measured
by the yardstick I put down in snow, by the wheel's curve,
and these hours at home, stirring, stoking the fire, running
water to wash all that is witnessed.

Home

I hear the names of the rivers,
their solemn declarations —
Assiniboine,
trees converging
on the Humber,
the Nechako fleeing a valley
where the temple kings
rose from the greening land.

There are truths divined
by moonlight.
There is a fire
near the doorway of a house
where a woman ponders
the dreams of wandering saints.

Are you one of these?
Are you a dream the elders
banished in their darkness?

The waves of the body grow quieter.
I am exiled, orphaned
like rain,
a brook melting steadily
into the black earth.

The eyes of your face behold the world,
behold those who weave on looms
emptied of light.

I arise broken.
Out of your body light pours,

the Euphrates rushing toward its homeland,
a meeting of messengers upon the waters.

◎◎

Her son from his room is listening.
The phone in her hand is the hallway
of a house he will enter.
It is the walled garden where a monk
contemplates a leaf.

Her son sees the foundation. Its hardness.
It is the palm of her right hand where
the phone rests. It is the story he begins
to tell.

'You will take me to a home
in a cul-de-sac,' he tells her.
'It is a house like summer.
The scent of lemon, geraniums,
the smell of cut grass and dandelion
scattered on the unpaved walk.

This I have also seen.'

It is as if evening had already arrived and obscured
the dimensions of a face. A house set back
from the road.

He sees the well with its steadied wheel,
her dress on a line shaken by the wind.

The road below. An easterly shooing the dust.

Perhaps it is the door he now knocks upon
out of thirst,
or the scattered bread
pecked at by migrating birds.

∾

Unable to speak, I lift up a stone and peer under.
The adobe house is now in darkness, smoke rising,
children striking out across the desert
in the old way. They become circles
that we are forbidden to follow,
the salt of a great city, the division
of an inland sea among its people.
We gather here together under the religion of stars,
each one an intersection, cul-de-sacs
of faith we set our books by.

I see the river in its absence, the ibis
praying to the still wet sky;
birch trees white as the robe she wore
into the water to find him.

It is as if a shutter flew open
and we emerged from a lasting sleep,
disturbing no one.

∾

At each parting your eyes reach for me, demand
love, rescue, demand what only

the destitute have come to know.

Please, I begin, *the music, listen.*

Your face is suffused, an evening lake
haunted by birds and gravity.

The trees outline something different in us.
Old throbbings, a bent treetop, the deepening
intensity of green. It is as if the waters of the earth
are also on fire around us.

I have come to fear the owl
that follows in my footsteps,
the grey sticks of the house,
the sounds night brings
when you are no longer with me.

     ◉◉

I return to the stove and stir.
Whichever way, I tell myself, *whichever way.*

As I stir, there is alchemy on the wind.
It drifts down the chimney,
does a turnabout on the kitchen floor
and pirouetting up to my chin
surprises the small boy
turning the spit for the evening meal.

How do you say goodbye?

There is part of me that goes travelling

and part of me that stays close to home.

Somewhere, all the rains have gathered under one sky —
I am on a road drenched to the skin.

The moon has prepared a shelter in her absence.

Tonight a fire is burning and the wind wanders
from door to door with its complaint.

Host

Faith comes from the ground, the faces of deer,
a coyote on the footpath looking warily
in two directions.

Pain is a lyrical host. It is the image of a house
falling into the earth, cast down, stoned
by its own people.

My son will never come home.

Repertoire of Longing

The Desire to Love a Man

Spring carries its repertoire of longing
like a pedlar who lifts his home on his back and walks
from door to door
singing.

I wake up alone.

There is some comfort in this, some grinding down of
a half-truth, the last light of a billion-year-old star
suddenly flaring as it dies.

Crows walking on the road look for signs:
a coat, feathers put on backwards, a man trudging
uphill, swaying under his implements
of rain.

I come home widowed after nightfall.

Soon, the bushes above the pond will glow like tree frogs
or fireflies that wander up and down the branches
looking for mates.

What I offer you is the small breath of a bird
who pecks at unfamiliar grain.

Remembering the Cottonwood

This is not a morning for birds. Geese in the hundreds pulling
the curtains across. I look out now that the light has come
back, and rebuild the cottonwood tree you cut down. But there
are no birds in it, only roots miles underground remembering
how you climbed the tree's back to find its weakening heart

and pierce it. That was the summer I wanted a garden. But, first
you unmade the tree and the tree's shadow. I swept blossoms of
cottonwood from my house for weeks after, picked them off
the dog's face, the children's lashes as they slept. I hid them in
the crawl space of the house, but the tree knew. In the darkness
that came after, she threw her great shadow over us, asking for
it all back.

This morning, this third day of March, I see the cracked earth
breathe out air that smells of mint I planted when you were
still here. Unliked by deer and the raccoon's young, it's replaced
the cottonwood's roots, forgotten her pure, unscented blossoms,
the way she hung over us, flinging her arms wildly at the house
whenever a foreign wind threatened to take us up.

Cape Spear, a Ballad

There is grass here that you can get close to, no matter what
season it is. Push back bramble and juniper, or snow. Part
the crowberry in midsummer and the earth beneath is a
partridge drunk with love. This is how I have always loved
you. A wave crashing on grey rock.

I lie on grass no higher than the hairs of your arm. The earth
tells me of your death, sings of your mercy, and repeats the
executioner's song. I rise and follow the path of a goldfinch
as he swings around the lighthouse road, ignoring the voice
calling him to come home.

There is refuge here, bunkers where years of your life may be
hidden away, folded with tender hands and placed inside a
silver box. It is what pirates do, or a captive who knows he is
about to die. I imagine a lock of hair under the closed lid, the
scapula of a sainted man who, crossing the ocean in a skin
boat, prayed for deliverance.

You are beside me, the scent of earth on your skin, your lips
cracked by salt and wind. The shadow of your hand spreads
over grass and slips through me. I am unseen, your guide, a
maker of words admonishing the sea for always taking you
back.

Divorced

The going home to moved furniture, the stubs of candles, the
 bed bearing only a smudge of you. There are years unaccounted
for, the ones where a lover's face is a father's perplexed by his own
slow death. This is how *you* left. Behind me as I shut the door.
Never too far away.

The dead are never far from us at all my sister said. She dreamt
of him one night, her face a rose in the pocket of his drowned
shirt. *Divorced* is what the water does to someone we will always
love, the bars on the window, moonlanes she swam down before
the earth fell away. Waking, she ran to search for the watch she'd
taken off his wrist after they pulled him from the lake. She found
the sky still making its quiet rounds through the house, the moon
tiptoeing about, seconds refusing to let up.

Lighting the fire, I think of the split wood, of how I've learned
to wield an axe and bring it down. The dog, watching nearby,
goes on chewing the gristle of his bone. I bend on one knee,
gather the stove lengths in my arms and take them inside.

Loneliness

There is a sudden loneliness that crosses the road
and walks uphill toward my house.
Perhaps it is the fog approaching, or the moon

only halfway here.
Loneliness is a luna moth
on fire inside the moon's yellow rings.

It is the moon with her unpowdered face,
the night-dewed grass closing over the antennae of a snail.

In May, tree frogs give off a scent I lean my upturned face into.
Lupines move slowly around the pond, darkness stumbling
alone through the twilight.

To see from the bottom up is to live many times.

Matilde

One morning I met my Matilde. How you must have loved her.
Your third wife. A heart big enough to carry all of you. Matilde
Urrutia. Your voice, so close to my ear, has her name for its
breath.

Going out for to view the fair fields. When you translated 'the
prince of light' was she the peace that came when the horse
was found weeping by the river?

She was dressed in the highest of fashion. Among the figureheads
of ships, her body became the country you loved, a mound
of earth that miners of salt go down into. Dawn sometimes
visited, the small gestures, the ocean pounding inside you.

And she wore in her hair a red rose. She was from the earth,
like you. A copper-coloured grain, golden maize shaped by a
healer's hands. At first, you disliked the roses she planted near
the house.

I stepped up and bid her good morning. You laughed when
they called you 'ambassador'. I was so poor, you said, there
was never enough food. But that was before Matilde, Spain,
the death of your tiny daughter, Malva Marina.

Her cheeks they did blush like a rose. One hundred songs
of love. You wrote in her blood, darkness burning with ink.
Names notched into the beams of the house sang for her, too.
Some days, Federico stood there looking at you, a brother
bursting to know.

Saying, Fair maid while the meadow is charming. She longed for
you, like a hummingbird remembering the nest her young had
been born in. *Your guider I'll be if you choose.*

Motherless Child

listening with Margaret to Paul Robeson

Sometimes, in the hollow bones of birds, the wind
feels its own solitary voice like a low rustle
moving down. A man is singing, *a long,
long way from home.* He is called
Paul because inside him is a church
of light, a pastorage equal to the feet
of a freed man.

Margaret lay in bed, absorbed by her own dying.
Her mother was taken away long ago
from the prairie house she grew up in.
On Tuesday nights, we'd play the record, sing
sometimes I feel,
while Margaret adjusted the morphine's gentle flow.

I sing *All through the night* as I prepare
my children for sleep. The voice of Paul Robeson
comes hurriedly to the door, home
from the prison where Miguel Hernandez
died, the Kremlin wall, a roaming band of gypsies
Hitler mistook for excavated earth
and let them sing.

Peace attend thee, my small voice says to Margaret,
already dead. To Paul Robeson,
on a high road, Loch Lomond, or the Oregon trail made holy
by a band of watching Cree.

O My Daughter

The river brings grebes whose song descends and is repeated.
They are sometimes heard in winter, or seasons without names
that my daughter has divided the year into. She sleeps now, and
I gaze into the fire to find the words to tell her the meaning of
"matrimonial" and "banish". Thinking of Eliot, the poem to his
daughter, I become *insubstantial, reduced by a wind.*

My daughter, a hummingbird has brushed its wing across your
face and touched you in sleep; a marriage. What glitters there is
your notebook of names for all that is shut out, discarded, the
messages we leave when night comes and we close the door.

I hear my voice become yours: the leaves our feet fall upon,
the crowns of so many trees that only sky can see, the fur of
a field mouse resting under a blade of grass. Each with its
story, lexicons of truth. Under a canopy of leaves a soothsayer
showed where his family will rest for the night. When we
winter on open water, our hearts are the bone dust of grebes,
floating nests regretful of the loss that is imminent.

A Good Death

i

A mouse the children pulled half alive from the cat's mouth
is lying on a bed of straw. From his bed in their cabin, his
black eyes are beautiful darts of starlight that form the vertical
tip of the Dipper's lid. They are searchlights sent out over
dismal waters by the lightkeeper's gentle son. The children
have placed him in a lined shoebox and covered him with a
lost glove. This morning, they are busy, attentive, preparing
for him a kindly death.

ii

The backbone of a dying man is an articulated bridge that
adjusts the flow of water when it suddenly swings free. Upon
his back, my hands know the imprint of secret sorrows like
an old conjuror rubbing a green stone in a smoke-filled room.
I utter the sick man's response, a slow moan that catches in
the mossy bark of trees or comes out curled and sad on Ward
10 South of the old infirmary. I am younger than anybody
else in here, a baby shuffling with baggy knees on the gleaming
floors. I am no longer like any of my former selves, so close
to his death, breathing in the way he does, a stranger, not kin
or friend just a man who sang by moonlight and graciously
asked me in.

After the Funeral

I have gathered together
all that is left of you.
I have opened books
you once rode through
toward the open sea.

But the books do not end
there: the sea was not the sea and you
came back to look me straight in the eye.

I have watched this long year
break away and dissolve.
I have watched the planets
pin themselves to your lapel.

My friend, I want to record
where you have gone,
how solitude enters through the sea wall
and is never washed away.

Gratitude

is a declension of love. I write *grateful, gratefulness* and think
of my mother at seventeen alone on a train, her infant
daughter dying in her arms. There is a word for the rain that
came, for the men who would not help. That night under a
rainblack sky, my grandfather brought his daughter home
on horseback.

In my grandmother's house, the dead child is finally taken
from my mother's arms. She will stay upstairs until summoned
to come down and sit near her father's side. She will remember
how we are set apart in our grief, and after a time, rise to
take a different chair, closer to the child's face. Her hands
will enfold, make steeples, fall away from the doorway of
the church as the tiny casket is slowly carried in.

The Last Time I Saw You

(for my father)

It all happened so fast. The maid calling down
the stairs, her voice was vapour-trailing
scarves of sunlight in early sixties' dots
yelling that you were dead: *gone,* she cried, *he's
gone.* Then dust motes, the stillness of the plum tree,
the hula hoop rolling to a stop in the driveway.

I know there were things I should have prepared
you for: those honeycombs of light that Kepler found
while dozing in his observatory;
the possibilities of dissolving like a moon,
or being struck dumb by starlight.

And now there is only this peripheral light
to look back with.
If I could tell you how it's been
these thirty-nine years,
it would be like hearing again that country song you once paid me
a silver dollar to sing.

A Woman in Flames

My mother's face is
a conspiracy of trees under moonlight.

It is the unnavigated ocean
mapped by a child's hand.

On it the Orinoco is a rivulet,
a watershed of exotic life ...
I see the greying institution of the chin
with its downward pull.

I see the night sky underwater,
the extravaganza of war,
a woman in flames at the water's edge.

Pilgrim

Your eyes are blue-
green lakes, glacial
ridges melting.

In your pupils,
mountain caverns and countries
never travelled.

I see joy and a hand waving.

The light has entered interiors
shaped by river over stone.

Your eyes are the sea
inside a loose, green veil.

I see passageways
through which you walk

and fields where
elk come home to sleep.

These are your eyes.

My child, the mountain
is turning, moving upstream.

The mountain is growing
a great jaw, shedding flesh

becoming bone, sinew;

she is performing dark acts.

Her heart is splayed in the moonlight,
her thighs enclose the moments of water,

baptismal, clear
as you are.

෧෧

O numinous night,
I have given you my son, my first-born.
I have consecrated the corners of the earth
with his going.

The hand I hold in mine is an allegory.
It is a hunter who sets out on a journey
to restore what has already been given.

At the bottom of his voice there are rivers
and canyons,
trees breaking into blossom,
a crow flying out of its own darkness
shadowing the moon.

I close the blinds of my house.

෧෧

My son, you have travelled far,
a pilgrim comforted by rain. What do you see

inside the darkness that unfolds like the passageways
of a hand? The night is bone and fire. A roadway
where travellers come to find each other.

The long scar of your body curves
the way a river does.
I have travelled its shoreline for days
tracking the cry of something wild
upon the water.

Since time and moonlight
you have moved inside me,
cleansed by fetal water.

I am a hidden womb where torches line
the corridors of stone and forgiveness
begins.

O sing for me, I cry, incant my weariness
into measured drops
until I become a lonely reed the wind
will play upon.

To My Children's Children

They lie beside each other with all their future sleeps
wrapped in so much dreaming. The snakes that were under
the bed forty years ago have shed many skins, are now thin as
nails. I believe they are those yellowed strands of grass under
the pile of wood not properly stacked for winter.

What shall I leave them to know me by? I have only small
stories to bequeath, vignettes of river drivers who, singing
over the roar of water, tilt their faces to the sky and run
down the spines of logs. Or the children of Lir turned into
swans by a stepmother's treachery. Nine hundred years. My
uncle loved a woman who saw dragons in her children's eyes
and lit fires at midnight on a snowy hill. In my garden, he is a
rusted weathervane forever pointing east.

After all night on the river, my children's eyes have become
more water than light. There are many places along its bank
to dwell, they tell me, pointing to the foundations begun, the
basements and upstairs bedrooms they walk toward to find
my children's children lifting their faces from sleep.

Winter Songs

I Think of the Masai in Winter

Light falls its different ways through snow. Late in the day the
sun flames from low-lying trees, the window streaming like a
lover's face. Where snow has lain untouched for days, there is
a pool of softer light that I once saw your dark hair give out.
I watch the herders who live there, Masai, their faces taller
than blades of grass. *Come closer*, they tell me, *remember this:*
to sacrifice a deer, sit in a circle and suffocate its sleeping
face. So that the blood is not spilled, nor taken away and lost.

Among teachers, the Masai walk. In the boardroom, they
demonstrate the meaning of conferencing. Masai men know
the sense of light, or a tribal order to marry and redeem the
offspring of last year's emaciated herd.

Snow and light are devices that bring me close to you.
Sometimes I stop on roadways lured by birds and other
shadows in the snowbanks left by hasty ploughs. The Masai
women hold hands in a light without shade, no memory of
me or you, nothing to disturb the reverie of their day but a
small goat, its bell, the red of their own faces, the brightness
of a dancer's shield.

Writing

From my bed, the way I've rearranged everything,
I can pull books easily from my shelf. Neruda's
beautiful song; Goyette's urn of ashes on the highway
after so many cups of tea. The new word I've learned
is there too, amanuensis, one employed
to take dictation or to copy manuscript.
I believe in the institution of the hand
and the old-time religion it preaches.
The tenth digit is a wave. The forefinger
instant fear.

From the Book of Job I learn that to be stricken
with death
is to enter a Bell Curve. So many chances,
ways to learn: my small son believes the wind
is God and that *she* speaks
a bilingual truth.

Tonight, a grey force is resting upon the Merrimac River
where Thoreau, wounded and alone, opens an *unroofed* book
dictated by the days of water moving under
his heart's blue shelf.

Composition in Winter

Fill a lost glove with light. Bow down under a passing crow,
and if its shadow touches your hand, wash it in moonlight
carried in a shepherd's purse. I imagine what is under snow
this way, the expeditions, a footprint waiting to melt. The
shepherd is a star in the Milky Way destined to die by
drowning. To scatter seeds that the birds have left behind. I
have seen a red-winged eagle with the body of a man; I've
touched his still throbbing side.

Light in Winter

Up North, men are driven mad trying
to discover where the earth hides it.

They find a house trussed up by the sea.
A man comes up the beach with nets that will
be thrown out, iridescent, to blossom underwater.

A grey light is held gently in the palm of one hand.

So many have come here, retraced footsteps:
there, a lover's ring fallen through the ice,
a strand of his hair from the lining of her coat.

At the window, she pushes the curtain aside
to see him more clearly, his heart the castings of a star
burning across the ages of sky.

The house sees in all directions, watches
as he hauls up his boat, her keel caressed
by the heaving, black slag.

The crusted-over rocks are huts with rooftops
made from moonlight. Their sheen makes her think
of crushing them, one foot raised,
the sea nearby bristling like radium.

Fire

In Nenets, fire goes by the name of *tu*. It is an old nomadic hunter, sometimes settling at the hearth of a woman whose husband will not be coming home. When marks of blood appear, fire moves on. The woman is alone for 'as long as the kettle boils'. This is star time, that which passes over the smoke hole at the centre of the tent. When fire leaves, she pulls her husband's sled outside in the snow and chops it up.

When she finishes packing, throwing away the twenty-year-old wedding cake, she wakes her children and tells them the old legends of childbirth. On the island where I was born, she says, an elderly aunt blew into the mouth of a newborn child to give it breath. The afterbirth lay untouched for many days, then was offered to birds to strengthen their migrating wings.

E-mail 1

Dear Sue,

This is not a poem.

I saw the picture of them standing under a tree, her head in the cranebill of his neck, him drinking her in, breathing just for her. So lovely as you say. Devotion. Divorce is what we chisel away from the centre, a garden grieving under snow. And then there are the abandoned places. *Did I say this is not a poem? Well, it isn't, really.*

I've read two essays this week, seen one play, and understand that to hear voices we must first learn to sing them. To see visions, we must look for the long way in. The long way. Like that angel you said the valley painter saw. Wounded. Left for dead. St. Brigid's flame burning without end. Did you know I lived in Ireland once?

I loved a boy there, a haunted mother's son. Her life was hell. In Canada, grieving for a loss is managed in a larger space. More sky. Especially where I'm from; that sea we talked of much wilder than the west. Those two in the picture loved for all they were worth, didn't they? Learning of it slowly the way a tree does.

I'd forgotten it was St. Patrick's Day. And the four-leaf clovers in the book I gave you, placed there twenty years ago. If you ever go to Ireland, you'll see your own face many times over, either standing in the Garden transfixed by the Children of Lir, or begging at the river for bread.

It's good to travel.

2 Dreams from a Boardroom

1.

I dream of snakes in a cage

The diamond-back is larger than all the others. In the classroom,
a boy shows me how we survive hurt the way a snake does, the way
diamonds grow brighter in the body's rough venom. Very good,
I say, weeping inwardly, wanting to close the curtains or open a
different book. He tells me he loves their geometric spines, the doors
they curl up against, the way their eyes go on watching from the
inside out. So, what has a boy got to do with the dream of snakes,
or the dream of a woman who stood outside the cage prodding
the wildness within?

2.

I think of my mother, and how she has the scent of rain

She has that smell of rain animals love. Rain tells the fur on their
backs to grow apart or upward, their eyes to see dark things when
the light is suddenly gone. Rain goes on falling through the morning,
tangling itself in the scent she loves me with. It is a hard, human
love, the one whose hair you cling to while rising from oceans you
were born in. But what of hope, and the terror of the wrist? And
what of the love I cannot love her with?

The Doorknob

I touch you briefly, leaving.
The roadway of my hand encloses
a valley, a circular ridge I sit upon
and contemplate

loss. Who were you, are you
now? What will endure of
this touching, these nights
searching for you in the darkness,
this sleeplessness?

As I write, the door of my room
moves gently in the breeze. I compose
lines of longing. For example, I write how
holding you I hold the world
in closing.

A Man I Know Who Can Talk about Light

The way light enters a house is the soul of the house, he
pronounces, the light upon him, the angle of his face, the
east wall which he imagines knocking down to let the eastern
quadrant of the sun come in. At the marriage feast, he is a
bridegroom offering ten square hectares for his bride's hand.

The man who can talk about light understands the carpenter's
touch, the need of an inventor to comfort a broken king.

The house he lives in is built so that the refractions of each
season will find it. The grainy light will sit all day on the
porch steps staring at the sky, shifting sideways when a friend
comes to join him. The light that winter brings is out there
now, filling the wings of snow angels, pacing back and forth,
running his bare hands over the north side of the haybarn to
warm them.

Fall comes. A straw hat resting against the sill, corn husks
darkening in the field. The light that passes the window is
old. It empties out of the room as the wedding guests prepare
to leave, as the son, who prays for the death of his father,
comes back home.

If we put our ear to the ground, light can be heard
approaching from a long way off. Sometimes, it is only one
rider we hear, his leather satchel slung over his shoulder, his
tired horse stopping to paw the chipped and dusty earth.

How Winter Came

We woke to ice on the pond,
upon the long stiffened necks of the sunflowers.
Their heads are bowed, regretful, awaiting
news of the fallen.

The moon came sliding down the hillside and
the children in their red dish careened out of sight
to carol among the still-darkened grasses.

Their faces are sunflowers searching the earth
for more light.

I stand at the window and search
for my own face in the perfect morning glass.
I lean closer into the years, beyond the laughter of
those I love who have come for me.

Are you me? I ask a child playing marbles on the road,
grinding the potholes of ice with her bare heel.

Outside, the garden tools stand perfectly still,
poised near the shed door like eloquent old men
whose beards have stiffened from long hours
in conversation around a coal fire.

Upon the window that separates us, I exhale
thoughts shaped like drifts of snow.

The children emerge from the half-light.
They show me icicles from the tailpipe of the car;
bits of see-through life from the eavestroughs;
the tin can with a frozen ship inside.

Now, they rush away, their bodies
swooping through the air, wings spread
their winter feathers trailing outward
searching for the place where ice grows.

Poetry and Snow

When I love you, each word in my head
is a *morceau* of polished, coloured glass,
a star swollen three times its normal size
as if sea water filled it.

The rain pools sit on the underside of the moon
that nobody has yet seen, nor walked down into.
All this water and loveliness. All this
praying over.

Such immensity! Snow goes on falling and yet there is
some pressing need the wind articulates. A man
wearing stars in his pillared hat once sat near the ocean
and drew circles and lines in the sand to show us
precisely where
his own confusion lay.

One night, windows thrown open under a winter sky,
Copernicus saw the shadow of his own hand fall
out of a star that was shaking inwardly with quiet light.

One night, suddenly awake, a stranger with shadowy
feet walked up to your door and knocked.
No one answered but the woman
who loves you, the dreaming one.
The hem of her white dress is all she left,
its image stamped forever upon the black universe of your
right eye.

Our own lives shine outward. We write
letters to friends who will never visit us but care that
our children are clean and safe. We visit shrines and cenotaphs
that are buried under ten feet of snow and brush away
for hours to find a hand. In this way, Rilke found Apollo
singing his maker's song.

E-mail 2

Dear Sue,

I forgot to tell you I'm going to make a kayak, double seater.
Forty hours, forty pounds, only need to know how to tie my
shoelaces. Great, eh? *How did you come to know those silences,
like baseball diamonds around which there is only the dark
emptiness of space?* And later in the summer, I'm planning
to get a vendor's license and sell Thai Noodle Salad down at
the harbourfront during the Busker's Festival. *Dort, wo man
Bucher verbrennt, verbrennt man am Ende auch Menschen.
All those ways to burn, running back to the house, your words
transliterated by shooting flames.* If I have enough time, I'd
like to take the ferry crossing to Port aux Basques, which
reminds me of the Basque whaling station dug up in Red
Bay, Labrador. Did you know? *That beetle with its casing
of air, is that a metaphor for the buoyancy of love, or the
transparency of our own growing faces?* When I get there,
I'll drive across the island and forbid myself to stop at
every glimpse of water, or every old highway grown over
with scrub. *When we are no longer hungry,* you said, *that's
when good things'll come.*

In Newfoundland the only roadkill is moose. I've seen
them butchered, and eaten for their capacity to outgrow us.
The Irish didn't think much of their meanderings until one
winter after all the potatoes had rotted in the root cellars,
they went tracking them as if they were giant elk with no
mind of their own. That was the forties and the war was on.
If I go down a sideroad on my way to St. John's, one might
pop up and surprise me. Imagine, like eating a dinosaur.

*The partridge lays eggs and hatches young birds who will never
follow it.* I also forgot to thank you for the books, and for the
many insightful ways you have of looking at a blank page.
When I get back, I'll take you out in the kayak.

Depression

is the shed door that opens and bangs shut
with only the smallest wind.

The door jamb and the threshold
of the door are permanently
curved as if from frost,
or from the old receding
cold that
will go only so far
away.

Depression is a body of
sadness, ecstasy
gone, the blindfolded child pinning
the donkey's tail
time after time to an empty wall.

The Scapegoat

i

Long ago, a man's bile was poured upon the head of a goat
and his body healed. A people corrupted by vineyards and
unbridled love sent one among them into the desert. They
removed his tongue so that the miracle of the goat god was
forever sanctified. *Azel,* they cried, *Azel,* glorifying his name.
In time, reptiles drew the shadow of the goat deep underground
where it wandered, waiting for light to appear.

ii

Gnosis is the prophet Mani, his body torn asunder by truth.
When snow blows across the windows of my house, it obliterates
the tree he sits in that overhangs the garden wall. This morning,
I hear him recounting the hours we have spent together in
conversation, singing his love for the light that is old and new.
A small snowdrift is creeping upward, reaching out to touch
the soles of his feet. The white of his face is pensive. He leans
toward me listening, an old wizard waiting for the riddle's
response.

iii

The scaffold under a newly risen sun threw out its arms to
bring him home. This is the dream of the condemned man:
to count the steps of his wealth, his house, his own brokenness.
When she opened the door thinking she heard her husband's
voice, a woman beheld a wheel spinning through space, a man
labouring inside it. He hammered on an anvil of steel, shaping
the feet of beasts that had served him in his infancy.

iv

A goat is grazing not far from where the moon has gone.
Under snow there are small grasses, crumpled moss. But
what do I know of this? Underground is where the soul
sleeps, wakes, distributes alms to the moneylenders who
wait near a fountain in the courtyard of a Tibetan king.

v

My daughter awoke from sleep, the moon crouching behind
snow-covered fir at the edge of the wood. She emerged
trembling from a past century, the words *adze* and *ochre* on
her lips. She said, others spoke, praising her goodness, held
forth the light she had carried with her into the windowless
houses of the dead.

vi

Tantalus suffered an everlasting thirst and bore witness.
When the son took his father's arms into battle, the stock-
brokers woke howling from their sleep. They kissed their
children and the darkness disappeared. Tantalus foresaw the
faith of Abraham, the stone slab he laid his son upon, the
sword poised to strike into the boy's heart, shimmering in
sunlight like a river. Snow fell. The herder wandering alone
on the hillside saw that night was coming and gathered his
goats under the overhanging boughs of an evergreen.

Watching My Daughter Sleeping

She is dreaming of the road. Seashells. The way rocks
at low tide let go of you, allow slippage, the sea taking you
back.

I want to go with her, pick the small stones
from her shoes, fill my pockets with them for the game
we'll play when she's older.

Remember, I begin, but she goes on sleeping,
the wind lifting her hair, small waves clawing the rocks
as the moon comes in to bring her home.

The days we spend
together are like this, waking to ourselves
from great distances, the water over our heads.

Blessings

Monday's child is fair of face. Born on this day, three wishes
are given. You may open a book to any page and witness
yourself illuminated tenfold. Yours is the face Leonardo
could not fathom, the brush stroke choked with light or
shadow where the window angled outward. The moon has
revealed an old blessing in you, one that heals travellers
who walk alone upon a road at nightfall.

Tuesday's child is full of Grace. Nothing but the riverkeeper's
promise will ever befall you. Siddhartha stood for forty days
watching the river take away the time he had spent beside
his beloved; the river brought it back on a pallet of reeds no
bigger than the stone he had skipped ten times over the waves.

Wednesday's child is full of woe. The Cathars carried the grail
of mysteries down from the mountains into a glacial sea.
Christ, they said, had wandered from land to land, working
first as an oceanographer measuring the depths of cities
hidden under shelves of stone. Grief comes whenever you
see migrating birds.

Thursday's child has far to go. The god of thunder bent down
and made manifest a house on a deserted roadway. In you,
oceans are subdivided and passed to your children's heirs.
Grieving is a story scribed by the one who walks beside you,
from dream to dream, along a broken path that leads away
from the house.

Friday's child is loving and giving. A father is loved and given
back, restored to the bloodline of his own truth. A radiance
touches you, discovers openings that the wind loves to feel.
When the goddess looked into her empty chalice, she saw
that your face had filled it, and the world to come was
emblazoned upon your skin.

Saturday's child works hard for a living. You stand on a chair to knead bread, carry hay, stack shelves in your father's store. When you play, it is always house, and the work never ends. Sometimes you are the minister in church, gesturing with your small hand, addressing the divine, anticipating the coming harvest when potatoes will have to be dug, or a pig chased down and killed.

But the child that is born on the Sabbath Day is a seeker of wisdom who finds the house, but hesitates to lift the latch. Inside, voices speak of his coming. He puts his ear to the door, listens awhile, then walks on to find the ferryman and cross the river.

Afterimages

The Horse of Uffington

Turn around three times in the eye of the horse.
Make a wish.

He will ride toward you or away, recede
or grow. The horse has no back for you
to sleep on. Only spine.

A chalk
face to stare at heaven with. To worship.

If I could turn prayer into spell, rib to ladder
and climb. Find the soul galloping
without its skin.

Spoon

is a sound that describes how the sea gives,
how it scoops the ungrown spines of invertebrates
from amniotic sacs to bead like mercury upon
a metal tongue;

is smaller than a shovel and far better for small hands
to dig with, to plunder the damp sand
covering the chalky heads of clams;

excavates the foundations of a city, builds waves
of asphalt where skateboarders glide at nightfall under a
spoon-shaped
moon;

frees the landscape from the shape of itself.

I consider the terminal points of the spoon, the properties:
it is a paddle turning moonwater, a spatula comprised of steel.
Under its skin the sky falls inward
and the face of the beloved is refracted, beautified
as before.

Spring Images

I step from the car onto a bridge whose small wooden beams
have been broken in places, splintered like bone.

A man is kneeling at the foot of his wife's
grave, his bowed head a small nest of sorrow.

He questions her. Asks for details of departure. 'There are so
many roads I don't know about,' he tells her, turning away.

This is the story the bridge tells: the way we say
forever in our sleep, or wake up on our knees praying to be
healed.

But how do we know the road if our feet never touch it?
The car is parked south of the cemetery gate, the door
refusing to open.

Springtime

Sing a Song of Roses. Spring is near. Under snow, grass is so much greener than I'd expected. The landscaped earth like the eyes of geese. Soon dandelions. Those claw roots to be dug up, boiled into a salve for excessive sorrowing.

A Pocket full of Posies. The garden has been gone forever. Somewhere the bulbs I planted are flexing like knuckles stiffened by labouring too long. There are grape hyacinths with skin bubbled purple from sobbing night after night; tulips remembered for the colour they crayon over brown mud.

Ashes, ashes. When cleaning the stove, I make sure the grey bone of fire is heaped far away from the house. Shroves are carried around the garden under a pale sky that wears a thumbprint of cinders upon its forehead.

We all fall down. On our knees in the washed-out streets. Still singing in a circle to find our way back.

To a Brother

I didn't know I loved the earth
can someone who hasn't worked the earth love it
I've never worked the earth
it must be my only Platonic love
        Nazim Hikmet from the poem
        "Things I didn't know I loved".

Have you heard how impossible it is
to give what you have so much of?
Have you heard of this? The inventories?
Touching you, my brother, is to know
the halfsweet breath of a puppy
whose girth is doubled by morning.

Did you know how much
you could really love this life,
the extension of space,
the last star to lose its face
before daybreak,
the woman who found you?

Have you heard that the country you live in
ends at the cul-de-sac of your street
and that your neighbour's fence is a border
confounded by dreaming?

Look up, it says, from its pickets and paint,
though somehow you cannot.
Somehow, you are a citizen of the fence,
of someone else's love,
of your own house where you are offered tea
by an old gypsy
who stops momentarily to sell you a cup.

Sare

She knew as much as Thoreau about the dispersal of seeds,
their canoe shapes, the soft prickles of the bakeapple leaves.
When the wind blew over the roof of her house, she smelled
the berries ripening on the bog. She knew where the wind
had settled their seeds, and, smiling to herself, planned the
days ahead for the picking, cleaning, and pots of golden jam.

Aunt Sare pulled on gaiters her husband wore. Rolling up her
hair, she took her berry bucket from a nail on the porch door,
then traipsed through the marshes where the bakeapples
grew. She sang her favourite hymns, sucked the late summer
air through squares of missing teeth, clucking at the wind.

I'd wait till she came home. I kicked at a stone or threw a ball
at the clapboard of our house. Then, crossing the road, past
chickens, the barn where the old horse Silver lived, I'd raise
my hand and pound upon her unlatched door.

My Song Is Always to You

There is so much goodness in you. You whisper into the ear of a man who has been denied food and drink in order to hasten his dying, so as not to judge, but to go on weighing darkness, or wake up with five poems of devotion in your hand. When you go into the world, you walk away from the footpath, your eyes a planetary exchange of light, emptying and filling like the moon in her dark, wintry grief.

In another land, the song I sing loosens the buffalo's chain, wades knee-deep in mud, longing for the way back. But you go about in quiet meditation. Your first thought is about the separation of water as it seeps to the root of a tree that has lived here for a thousand years. What lived here before that, and before that? you ask. And the water goes on falling, transparent.

The goodness in you is the dual morphology of trees. Rings of light, orbits around the body's deep centre. There are trails cut through forests that are packed down with decomposing seas. Trilobites, the skeletons of ferns that once waved their high plumes over the riverkeeper's hut. And what did you discover riding there before you followed the river's path? Three dark sins, one surely a crime that had climbed off the horse and opened the keeper's gate.

A Small Girl Playing with Horses

The big horse is a girl like her, fetlocks cooling in the damp
Dakota grass, the mane overfull like a small daughter's braid.
The dark one gallops fast. He is Geronimo in the saddle
dreaming of a circus and the performance of three sorrowful
acts. Then, chaos drops its dark cape at the river. They stop
and bend with eloquent knees to drink the Rio Grande dry.
Such thirst.

On the other side, there are twenty-two teepees in an Apache
camp. Their eyes follow her face, the little cup of her lips
releasing its soft *giddyup,* lullaby of a riverbank. The others
follow, the grey, the dappled, the Arabian foal spindly as a
river reed. She lines them up, gallops on the dark one's back,
up and down the ranks inspecting, advancing, digging in.
A war where nobody came. Only horses eating the singed,
August grass.

The horizon is no longer where she first placed it. And a
valley has appeared with buffalo thundering full speed
toward train tracks, to the edge of a town where sheriffs with
tarnished skin walk among horses wearing suits of wavering
silk. *Giddyup,* she whispers in the dark one's ear, as if home
with its fires was a direction the horse could already see.

Sometimes, when she isn't looking, one horse can be seen
praying for another, or for the Apache brave who walks alone
into a fort with only his dream to protect him. He throws his
blanket over the dark one's back, lifts her up to sit behind
him, and tossing his night-black hair, gallops forward into
sleep.

True Love

Walk Up and Down the Valley. The wind blowing. I have hair
that is written about in books: Sally's or Jane's, yellow and
uncompromising. Now we hold hands in a circle that spreads
over the hill above the school. My grandmother says a circle
is both holy and damned, depends on who's inside it. *'Til the
Highland Gates are Closed.*

Kneel Down Before Your True Love. The one inside looks
around for a face to match her own. I squeeze my toes
together and pray to be chosen. To be in the future with a
husband who rides horses and understands the computational
way stars maneuver to find light. The breath of his horse is
the wind nuzzling my back, urging me toward the centre.
'Til the Highland Gates are Closed.

Stand up and Say You Love Her. When he comes for me, the
ribbons tying my hair will spell his name, dark like a river.
Perhaps I'll ride away seated sideways, lock the small door
and leave. When they come to look for me, what will they
find? Clumps of the horse's mane on the fence we rested
against, dreaming of sleep. *'Til the Highland Gates are Closed.*

Go In and Out the Window. Taiga is the colour of a Fox
Sparrow, her breast is a map painted by a Cherokee brave
depicting the slow arrival of his people. I imagine that only
bluebirds can weave as steadily as this, the way our feet always
land on horsetail and weedy grass. *'Til the Highland Gates are
Closed.*

Go Follow Her to London. The horse draws near the city's
west end, Old Chelsea, Bunhill-in-the-Field where I will sit
before the grave of a poet who died in a fiery vision of himself.
Suddenly, I hear my mother's voice with its aroma of bread
and boiled meat. I sing higher than the others, rake my hands
over the horse's tired back, a lover unused to want. *'Til the
Highland Gates are Closed.*

Arianna Standing on a Stone in the River

Spring water moves with fury and stealth.
It has wingbeats upon its breath, and right here
where her feet rise out of its body, the clouds
have moved apart and light gathers
slowly in. She is the water's green edge
visible again after ice has moved off, clamouring,
jousting all the way down
into Bedford Basin.

Up here, the river clears its throat and sings
Aria Aria
in loose tremolo, polydactylic phrases,
until she hears all at once
the story of how she came to be here
tears running down her face
as she wades in midstream.

Water loosens the furze-entangled heart, pours
it out, the jar of it a boat
with bulging ribs. So many messages
reach us that we cannot decipher. The wash of water,
for instance, is telling her to lean
over its surface and find her face.

She will not leave.

The hat she wears is a rainbow
with curled, secret edges.
Above her, the song of a bird recalls
a journey begun somewhere in the fourth
century, the story of a murdered girl,
children lost in a great forest trying
to reach home.

Look down, the story continues, and search
for the distances glimmering
under the water's bill.

A Bear Foraging through Broken Woodland

There is as much sniffing as you said there would be
though the bear didn't at first see us. She walked
past me as if I wasn't even there. Was I? Is this
the same dream again that has woken me, that
finds me now going home on a rain-enchanted road
wondering what your warning really meant after all?

Seduced by your bear voice, your berry-scented
hands, I searched the stacks for Thoreau
in his unpainted house on Walden Pond, where he sits
after a day hammering and singing
in conversation with you. You crack another *beer* and laugh
because it sounds
like *bear* and you know she is sniffing around
just outside the door.

The Green Man

One day he walked straight
out of the river wearing a
green suit. One day

I looked up and he was leaning
his long body over the brink
of my white shoulder. His voice

was water — green sounds — aqua tints

(*but death has such tiny feet,*
such delicate prints, you said)

He came out of the river wearing a green suit.
He removed the underwing of a dark bird
and changed the wallpaper
because he was afraid.

Fear is a dark bird

Because he was afraid he lay down
in my arms under the crushing weight
of leaves and whispered:

the river has a legend you should know

River Images for My Son

In March the river rises. On its bank
the thin bodies of birch reach up, herons stretching
a paper-maker's wife pounding
reeds in the wind.

We hold the wind in our hands and count.

In my son's hands feathers begin
to multiply. He gathers them inside the snowy
continent of his heart, their histories
and maps carefully laid out.

One day, he says, a falconer stumbled upon
an ancient grave and looked into
the face of his beloved. His steady hand afire in the sun,
the memory of her kept alive, catalogued
by touch.

It is as if we have been sought after but have waited too long.

What befalls me in the daylight
is this certainty: the river at my feet, stones where
the vocabulary of change is constantly
washed clean, my son's face
upstream in the steady, untilled current.

The river is higher than the hats the children wear.
The rock they stand on. I bend low,

my ear in their conversation
and find no way out.

Kneel here, they say, our hands together. *Listen.*
The river, a silhouette, *listen*: the ambushed heart.

๑๑

Yours is the after-image of a face,
a stone the river washes upon
when asking to leave.

What memories will you take of me?
Night has a scent
all its own. Water, its own
inventories.

If I could lure the moon
from its bed beside you.
If I could convince myself
there are ten thousand ways
to look back.

๑๑

The river water is the colour of sorrow.
A child finally leaving home.
I place my cheek on stone and hear
the lament of an ocean.

How is this possible? I ask.

I kneel before the river,
the salt of an ocean on my tongue.

O Lamentations.

There are stones your feet
have never touched,
nets that have rested for centuries
on the river bottom.

The sea fills, empties, welcomes
the vast migration of birds that navigate
estuaries and marshes
to find new life.

&

One day, a valley man returned from his field. Dusk came.
Unsatisfied, he wandered in an orchard
to pray alone.

In the same way, we enter cities.

The river finds my hand and fills it
over and over again. Sometimes, it is the sky
I feel in my palm, or the ashes of
a star spilled from its silent urn.

&

During the long night
I walk here, the moon a mantra.
Sometimes I dream the river
into miles of mangrove,
and wander lost for days.

The children wade upstream

and send their small boats
to find me.

But you, my eldest,
have only a tiny raft
drifting
under a haiku wind.

಄

Upon the floodplains, morning
is a decoy of birds, the egret
resting on the water's edge
waiting for her young to come home.

Each time we come here,
remove our coats,
assemble near the shore
an entire civilization appears.

The tents of excavators go up,
surround a city wall, a pyramid
where the feather of an egret
lies in the palm of a dying king.

Where is the father who never loved us?

His face, the river bottom, his memory of them
a particle of light.

On the Yangtze, a boy maneuvers
his small boat alone. The river, he believes,

is the birth water of an ancient bird.
Each day he sails downstream
her bright wing nestled against
the softness of his cheek.

When giving birth, a camel lies down
at the feet of a herder and weeps.
This is the place of water.

*We are devoted to the dying. To the unloved, the children
we do not know.*

❀

The manatee searches the river
unearthing stones to find her young.

Once when the river rose so high
she found a nest floating upon a wave
and wept. *Bring them back,* she demanded,
bring them back.

If you look long enough, a stone will move
the moment you turn away.

The depth of the river is measured by its own journey.
Sturgeon a century old.
The manatee going upriver, her young,
unweaned and still.

❀

You sit before me in candlelight,
your face poured out like water.
You are the son who came back,
bidden home as the river rises
to flood estuaries and darken
the knees of wandering birds.

ⓔⓔ

On the banks of the Euphrates they tallied
their losses — cattle gone astray, goats
that wandered off into the night,
twenty horses galloping up the hillside
never heard of again.

If I could tell them.

There are new eggs that will hatch by morning,
the child who wanders along the riverbank
looking for a way to cross over.

Faith.

Once, when the river was so high, the ibis carried
her nest for days fearful should one egg be lost.
Carry me, too, she cried. And the boy
lifted her into his arms without once
looking back.

ⓔⓔ

The river returns to us.
The manatee to her solitude,
the eagle
to her nest on a rise of land
above the river bed.

My hand in water ripples the thin
surface. Slow
dissolution. A sea turtle
bearing the sky.

What is it we carry
that cannot be set down?

The scarf I weave is a river
where an explorer lived out the end
of his days.
It is the malaise of winter,
the green strip of courtesy that divides
mountains.

Overhead, the sky goes on as before,
children
tumbling in the air over a new
continent.

My son, I offer you now
a winding river of starlight, buckled
like a mapmaker's tear.

Notes

"John" is for John Saunders, a wonderful man and teacher. Platero is a reference to Juan Ramon Jimenez's donkey of the same name for whom he wrote *Platero and I*. The book was dedicated to the crazy girl Aguedilla.

Matilde was Neruda's wife Matilde Urrutia. The song lyrics framing the stanzas are a traditional Newfoundland folksong collected by the author.

"*O my daughter*" was inspired by T.S. Eliot's poem "Marina." The italicized words are quoted directly from the poem.

"Song of the Beloved" is for the Newfoundland artist Dave Panting.

"E-mail 1" and "E-Mail 2" are for Sue Goyette who inspired me to write them. In "E-mail 2", the German is from Heinrich Heine and translates roughly as *wherever they burn books they will in the end burn human beings*.

"A Man I Know Who Can Talk about Light" is for Bob Shields.

"Springtime". In different church traditions the word "shroves" was sometimes used to refer to the pancakes eaten on Shrove Tuesday, or the unspecified offering burnt in a "Shrovarium" (so that sinners would be "shriven"), the ashes of which were dabbed on the forehead the next day. "Bringing in the Shroves" was also sung in Shrove Tuesday processions. Indeed, the true nature of shroves is a mystery, as many clergy have suggested, and largely "a matter of faith."

"My Song Is Always to You" is for my sister Ramona.

"True Love." The children's game song framing the sections of the poems is from my own childhood.

"A Bear Foraging through Broken Woodland" was inspired by Don McKay's workshop on wilderness at Gaspereau Press.

Acknowledgments

I would like to thank the editors of *The Fiddlehead, TickleAce, Vintage '94* and *'95, Running the Goat Press* and *ARC* where versions of some of these poems were originally published.

My heartfelt thanks to Sue Goyette for her support, encouragement, careful reading of the poems, and unparalleled insightfulness. The laughter was so healing.

Thanks especially to Catherine for making the years it took to write these poems more bearable, and for bringing a needed dimension of levity with the generosity and depth of her spirit. Our marvelous winter of Friday nights around a fire fair cured my melancholy.

To Blair, for the friendship.

Thank you, thank you to my wonderful children for inspiring me in their innocence, and for putting up with me during manic creativity and the despair and frustration of editing; to my parents for seeing me through an especially tough east coast winter; to brothers and sisters for whom some of these poems were written; and to my sister-in-law Andria Hill Lehr for her wild, gracious spirit.

My appreciation goes to Jane Buss and the Writer's Federation of Nova Scotia for their support and encouragement. Thank you so much for selecting me for the inaugural writing mentorship program that truly changed my life.

Thank you to Kitty Lewis and everyone at Brick Books, and to my wonderful editor Elizabeth Philips whose thoughtful attention to the poems teased out the knots and the light.

Finally, I'd like to extend my thanks to Marnie Parsons for publishing ten of these poems in the chapbook *The Design of Wings*, Running the Goat Press, St. John's, Newfoundland. Thank you Marnie.

Genevieve Lehr lives in the Halifax area and teaches in the public school system. With Anita Best, Lehr collected and compiled *Come and I Will Sing You: A Newfoundland Songbook* (University of Toronto Press, 1985; reissued with a new preface 2003). *The Sorrowing House* is her first collection of poetry.